Malcolm Arnold

SYMPHONY NO. 5, Op. 74
(1960)

Edited with a
2003 edition

NOVELLO

Order no. NOV 890202

Music set by Woodrow

This edition © Copyright 2003 Novello & Company Ltd.
Published in Great Britain by Novello Publishing Limited

Head office: 14/15 Berners Street, LONDON W1T 3LJ, England.

Sales and Hire:
Music Sales Distribution Centre, Newmarket Road,
Bury St Edmunds, Suffolk IP33 3YB

Tel. +44 (0)1284 702600
Fax +44 (0)1284 768301

www.chesternovello.com
e-mail: music@musicsales.co.uk

All Rights reserved

Printed in Great Britain

No part of this publication may be copied or reproduced
in any form or by any means without the prior
permission of Novello & Company Limited.

Malcolm Arnold · SYMPHONY No. 5, Op. 74

Commissioned by the Cheltenham Festival Society, Malcolm Arnold's Fifth Symphony, Op. 74, was composed in 1960. The work was first performed at the Town Hall, Cheltenham on 3 July 1961 (the year of Arnold's fortieth birthday), almost ten years to the day after the première of his First Symphony at the same venue; as in July 1951, the composer conducted the Hallé Orchestra. Ten years elapsed, though, before the Fifth had its London première, on 16 December 1971 (shortly after Arnold's fiftieth birthday); it was performed at the Royal Festival Hall by the New Philharmonia Orchestra. It is fitting, then, that this new edition of the Symphony should herald another anniversary: Arnold's eightieth birthday.

Malcolm Arnold composed the Fifth Symphony towards the end of a period of intense compositional activity. His output during the previous decade – the years immediately following his departure from the London Philharmonic Orchestra as principal trumpet – had included not only the four earlier symphonies, but also a stream of concertos, orchestral works, chamber music, suites and ballets. In addition, Arnold had established a formidable reputation in the genre of film music, his score for *The Bridge on the River Kwai* (1957) having won him an Oscar.

Yet his increasing prestige supplied an ineffective shield against criticism of his essentially conservative, pragmatic musical idiom. The Fifth Symphony was particularly controversial. In an age unsympathetic to any serious musical dalliance with 'neo-romanticism', the Fifth earned Arnold 'a black mark for putting a tune into a symphony' – to borrow the words of one contemporary headline. The 'tune' which essentially caused the fuss was the opening subject of the second movement. This string melody shocked not only because of its lyrically balanced phrases and diatonicism (a feature which was accentuated by the chromatic inflexions); more audacious still was the theme's climactic reappearance at the end of the final movement. This apotheosis prompted one commentator to style the theme as pure 'Hollywood'. The London *Times* found the melody 'embarrassing', likening it to the efforts of 'MacDowell'. Jeremy Noble, writing in the *Musical Times*, more generally compared the work to other 'jolly neo-romantic confections' of the period. And, under the caption '"Hit tunes" in new work at Festival', the *Gloucestershire Echo* recorded that even whilst the 'thunderous applause' had reverberated around the Town Hall, 'other sounds could be heard – the sharpening of critical knives and the baring of critical talons'. These weapons were doubtless exhibited during the 'fierce' debate that ensued in the Festival Club.

The possibility that the Symphony's musical language might have been laced with irony figured surprisingly little in contemporary notices. Yet an inkling of Arnold's more complex intentions is evident in his programme note for the first performance. In the third of his four sentences, Arnold wrote, cryptically: 'It will be noted that in the second movement the composer is unable to distinguish between sentiment and sentimentality.' He later enlarged on this, in a letter quoted in John S. Weissmann's note for the London première. The second movement is a 'simple emotional cliché', Arnold explained; 'The point that I was trying to make in this work was the fact that we all, in great emotional crises, express ourselves in the simplest of clichés, and from my study of music I have seen that this applies to music also.' He added that 'the first movement was brought about by thoughts of so many of my good friends who have died very young ... To really drive home my point of view the whole piece ends with a statement of the theme of the second movement'.

In this light, the Fifth Symphony amounts to much more than the 'Saturday night Proms' number that one critic took it to be. For, in conjunction with its resourceful symphonic processes (the evolution of much of the first movement from a series of symmetrical four-note chords, for instance), the music subtly explores, blends, and juxtaposes ironic, ambiguous, and often conflicting modes of discourse. The grandiose return of the second-movement theme in the final movement is a case in point: it is far from the easy, triumphal statement it initially seems. In the first place, the dominant thirteenth that ushers its entry is too garish to be heard as anything other than an aural quotation mark. Then, denied its proper ending, the theme grotesquely lurches into the 'wrong' key. Finally, its texture spectacularly deflates, leaving a disturbing void. The posited 'triumph' has not merely evaporated; it has been negated.

For this new edition, I have clarified aspects of Arnold's notation and corrected indisputable errors and omissions. I have not, however, imposed consistency and conformity in details such as phrasing and articulation as a matter of policy. Rather, I have followed a more flexible scheme that aims at conserving Arnold's original notation in those instances where it might impact upon the musical meaning.

MILLAN SACHANIA
London, 2000

Addendum (2003 edition)
Although the autograph manuscript of the Fifth Symphony indicates a completion date of 7 May 1960, Arnold stated that he wrote the work in 1961 in a letter cited in Weissmann's programme note for the London première (1971). It may be of interest that Paul R. W. Jackson has recently suggested other factors that might support a completion date of 1961 (see his *The Life and Music of Sir Malcolm Arnold: The Brilliant and the Dark* (Aldershot, 2003), pp. 106–7).

The 2003 edition of the Fifth Symphony corrects some misprints in the 2000 edition; I am grateful to Paul Mann for bringing a number of them to my attention.

M. S.
London, 2003

Contents

I   Tempestuoso   *1*
II Andante con moto   *60*
III Con fuoco   *86*
IV Risoluto   *128*

Instrumentation

Piccolo
2 Flutes (Fl. II doubling Piccolo II)
2 Oboes
2 Clarinets in B flat
2 Bassoons

4 Horns in F
3 Trumpets in B flat
2 Tenor Trombones
Bass Trombone
Tuba

Timpani

Percussion (2 players):
Cymbals
Suspended cymbal
Side Drum
Bass Drum
Tam-tam
Bongos
Deep Tom-tom
Glockenspiel
Tubular Bells (treble G and B)

Celesta

Harp

Strings

Duration: 33 minutes

SYMPHONY No. 5

I

Malcolm Arnold, Op. 74

© 1960 Paterson's Publications Ltd.
This edition © 2003 Novello & Company Limited.

All rights reserved
Printed in England

26

30

56

II

III

96

112

116

118

122

IV

148

153

158